The People of St Lucia

HODDER
Wayland

an imprint of Hodder Children's Books

THE PEOPLE OF ST LUCIA
THE LANDSCAPE OF ST LUCIA

Cover: Background: People enjoying the sunshine on a beach on the west coast.
Inset: These two brothers are the best of friends.
Title page: Gladys Bauta, a trader at Castries market, sells some fruit and vegetables.
Imprint page: A single-storey house in Anse la Raye.

Series editor: Katie Orchard
Designers: Sterling Associates (cover) and Mark Whitchurch (insides)

Picture Acknowledgements:
All photographs are by Jeremy Horner except Eye Ubiquitous 6 (E. Atkinson), 24 (Bruce Adams); Hutchison Picture Library 29 (J. Henderson); St Lucia Tourist Board 27. All map artwork is by Peter Bull. Line artwork on the cover and repeated on the inside design is by Jan Sterling.

First published in 1998 by
Wayland Publishers Limited
This edition published
in 2001 by
Hodder Wayland

The author wishes to thank Alison Corfield and Nigel File for providing additional information.

© Hodder Wayland 1998

British Library Cataloguing in Publication Data
Brownlie, Alison
The people of St Lucia. – (From the heart of the Caribbean)
1. Saint Lucia – Social life and customs – Juvenile literature
I. Title
972.9'843

ISBN 0 7502 3823 2

Typeset by Mark Whitchurch, England
Printed and bound by
G. Canale & S.p.A., Italy.

Contents

Introducing St Lucia

St Lucia is a small Caribbean island with a long and interesting history. The first peoples to live here were the Caribs and Arawaks, who came from South America. During the seventeenth and eighteenth centuries, the French and British arrived on St Lucia. The island changed hands no fewer than fourteen times as the British and French fought bitterly to control it.

▼ There are bus services around the island. Sometimes it is quicker and cheaper to hitch a lift on the back of a neighbour's truck.

TIME LINE

1500s	St Lucia is shown on maps for the first time.
1667–1796	The British and French fight over the island. It changes hands 14 times.
1814	St Lucia comes under British rule.
1979	The island gains independence. It remains in the British Commonwealth.
1990	St Lucia, Dominica, Grenada and St Vincent discuss forming a Windward Islands Federation.

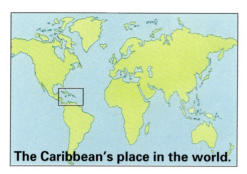

The Caribbean's place in the world.

St Lucia → St Lucia's place in the Caribbean.

Some descendants of the original Caribs still live in St Lucia. But most people are descended from Africans, brought over during the eighteenth century by the British to work as slaves on sugar plantations. Later, people came to St Lucia from India and the Middle East to find work. Today, the island has a rich mixture of peoples and cultures.

Clues about St Lucia's past can be seen all over the island. Many old buildings look similar to French buildings. But people drive on the left like they do in Britain. People in rural areas use similar farming methods to those used in parts of West Africa. St Lucians speak *patois* or Creole, a mixture of French, English and African languages. The official language is English.

PEOPLE FACTS

Population: 140,000

Capital: Castries

People: 90 per cent African descent, 6 per cent mixed, 3 per cent East Indian.

Currency: Eastern Caribbean Dollar ($EC), known as the 'ecee'. 4 $EC is £1.00.

N

Gros Islet

Vigie Airport

CASTRIES

Anse La Raye

Soufrière

Mount Gimie ▲

▲ *Petit Piton*

▲ *Gros Piton*

Hewanorra Airport

Vieux Fort

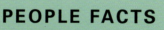
0 1 2 3 4 5km

Key
— Roads
✈ Airports
🎭 Carnival Towns

Family Life

Families and community life are very important to people in St Lucia. Many families on the island are quite large. It is not unusual for a family to have four or more children.

In rural areas, children often help their parents when there is a lot of work to be done. Neighbours and friends help each other out, too, especially when times are hard.

Extended Families

Often, grandparents and other members of the family, such as uncles and aunts, all live together in the same house. This is called an extended family. There are no old people's homes in St Lucia, because elderly people are usually looked after by their families.

Children are brought up to ▶ look after their younger brothers and sisters, and to help out around the home.

◀ St Lucian families spend a lot of time together.

▲ With so many beautiful beaches, families often spend a day by the sea at weekends.

Relatives in Faraway Places

Over the years, many people have left St Lucia to look for work abroad. In the 1950s, many went to live in Britain. They were attracted by the offer of jobs from the British government to work in London and other large cities.

Other people have migrated to the USA, Canada, and other Caribbean islands, such as Martinique and Trinidad, to look for work. So today nearly every family in St Lucia has at least one relative who lives abroad.

Keeping in Touch

Families in St Lucia like to stay in touch with each other. People who work abroad send money back home to their families as often as they can. Many people who now live in Castries used to live in small villages in the countryside. They still have relatives there and visit their families at weekends.

CASE STUDY

The Louis Family

The Louis family live in Anse la Raye. Marvin is a fisherman and part-time builder. Lisa looks after their two children, Helen and James. Helen is three years old and James is eight months old. The children's grandparents live close by.

'Lisa and I both come from large families. We want Helen and James to have lots of brothers and sisters to play with,' says Marvin.

▼ **The Louis family outside their home.**

Home Life

St Lucia is a hilly island, so it is difficult to find flat land on which to build. On the steepest land building is simply impossible. But people do manage to build houses in the most awkward positions.

Homes on Stilts

All over St Lucia, houses are perched on the sides of steep valleys. To make the floors level, many houses are built on stilts. The space beneath is often used for storage or made into an extra room. Even some houses on flat land are built on stilts. When it rains heavily, water can run underneath these houses so they do not get flooded.

▼ **These houses on stilts, just outside Castries, have been built on the side of a steep hill.**

▲ Clouds gather over an old wooden house in Anse la Raye. Its steeply pitched roof will allow the rain to run off quickly.

Building Materials

Homes in St Lucia are designed to cope with the warm, moist climate. The walls of most houses are made from wood or breeze blocks. Roofs are usually made from tiles or galvanized iron, which makes a lot of noise when heavy rain falls on it. Most houses also have pitched roofs, which are very steep to allow the rain to flow off easily.

FACILITIES IN ST LUCIA

Cinemas: 1
Radio stations: 4
Hospitals: 5
Private telephones: 26,000
Private cars: 9,000

Town and Country Homes

Most people in St Lucia live in houses rather than flats. Wealthy people live in large homes, but most are small, single-storey buildings. Nearly every house has a veranda. St Lucians enjoy sitting outside on warm evenings, chatting about the events of the day.

In large towns, such as Castries and Vieux Fort, most homes have televisions, washing machines, microwaves and running water. But in rural homes there are fewer luxury items and instead of televisions people rely on radios for entertainment. In most villages, people collect their water from standpipes in the street. The warm climate encourages people to spend a lot of time outside, especially doing jobs such as washing clothes.

▼ **This woman is keeping cool in the shade of her veranda.**

◀ In Castries there are several fine old houses. But most people live in homes that are much less grand.

Gardens and Vegetable Plots

Gardens with lawns and flowers are only found around larger houses in Castries and its suburbs. In rural areas, people grow their own food on small plots of land. They grow fruit and vegetables, such as mangoes and sweet potatoes. Any food that they do not need is taken to the market in Castries to be sold.

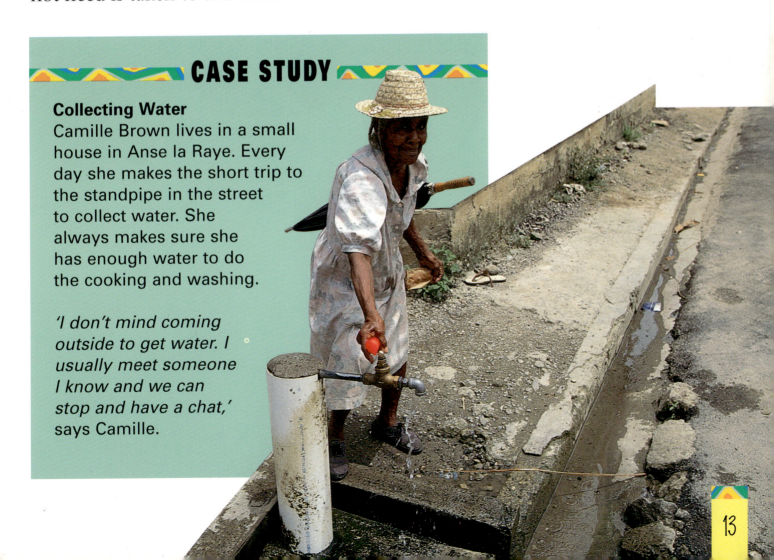

CASE STUDY

Collecting Water

Camille Brown lives in a small house in Anse la Raye. Every day she makes the short trip to the standpipe in the street to collect water. She always makes sure she has enough water to do the cooking and washing.

'I don't mind coming outside to get water. I usually meet someone I know and we can stop and have a chat,' says Camille.

Food and Cooking

All the different groups of people who have come to St Lucia have each brought their own styles of cooking to the island. They have also contributed something to the crops that are grown here.

Growing Food

St Lucia has the perfect climate for growing juicy fruit, such as pineapples, paw paws, mangoes and passionfruit. Vegetables, such as sweet potatoes, breadfruit, plantain, yams and cabbages also thrive on the island. Fresh fish and seafood are caught daily in the sea surrounding St Lucia. So people on the island are able to eat a well-balanced and healthy diet.

▼ People sip refreshing coconut water which they have bought from this street vendor.

▲ This man prepares to harvest his small garden crop with a machete.

Many people grow their own fruit and vegetables. Even in the towns people sometimes have small plots of land in their gardens so that they can grow their own food.

BAKED BANANAS

You will need:

125g butter

4 large, ripe bananas

250g light brown soft sugar

125 ml lime juice

2 teaspoons ground allspice

Butter an ovenproof dish. Then arrange the bananas in a single layer. Sprinkle the sugar on top. Mix the lime juice with the allspice and pour it over the bananas. Ask an adult to help you bake the dish at a medium heat for 15 minutes. Serve the bananas hot with cream.

Buying Food

Food that cannot be grown on the island is bought from the markets, or in Castries, from the supermarkets. Rice and flour have to be imported from other countries. Imported food can be very expensive. Castries also has a few fast-food shops. But a cool, refreshing drink of coconut water from a fresh coconut is still a popular treat.

Popular Dishes

A typical meal for St Lucians is fried plantain or pounded yam, with a pepperpot stew. Spicy curries, fish soups and poached fish make a tasty change. The national dish is a special kind of soup made from *callaloo*, a type of spinach.

▲ **Fruit and vegetables for sale in Castries market.**

▼ **Roadside huts such as this one provide quick snacks and drinks for hungry passers by.**

16

Market Day

On market day in Castries, Gladys Bauta sets up her fruit and vegetable stall. Gladys belongs to a co-operative. Once a week, Gladys and the other members of the co-operative load up a van with the fruit and vegetables that they have grown in their small gardens. Each week a different member of the co-operative agrees to look after the market stall.

'It's a hard life, but I don't complain. We all help each other out,' says Gladys.

School and Play

All children up to the age of eleven in St Lucia go to primary school. Although many of the children speak Creole at home, the lessons are always taught in English.

Sitting Exams

At the age of eleven, children have to pass an entrance exam to get into secondary school. A lot of the children have extra lessons to prepare them for the exam. Some children have to help their parents on the family farm when they are old enough, so it is very difficult for them to continue their education after primary school.

▼ **All schoolchildren in St Lucia wear uniforms.**

Carmen René School

Carmen René School is a primary school in Castries, with about 400 children. The classes are quite crowded, with more than 30 children in each class. The children are lucky because they can go on study trips to the rain forest and the volcano to learn about their environment.

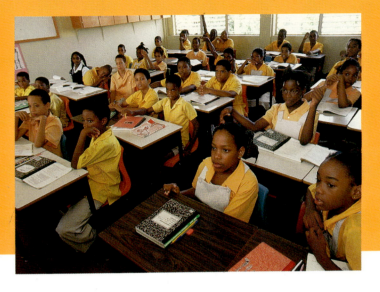

▲ A classroom at Carmen René School.

Secondary School

There are not many secondary schools in St Lucia, so the classes are usually large. Children are taught English, maths, science and social studies. Many learn to play a musical instrument, and schools often hold a concert at the end of term. Some schools have links with schools in Britain. The children write to each other about their schools and where they live.

◄ Sometimes, when the weather is hot, the children have some of their lessons outside under the trees.

Time to Relax

Young people in St Lucia's towns watch quite a lot of television. US soap operas, in particular, have become very popular. Children all over St Lucia also like to listen to the radio. Some radio stations broadcast in Creole. Sports are popular in St Lucia, too, especially cricket. For those who can afford the expensive equipment, there are plenty of water sports to choose from, such as water skiing, windsurfing and volleyball.

▼ **These girls are enjoying a game of elastics in the playground after school.**

▲ **Three times a week, villagers in Anse la Raye get together for a football match.**

Tim-Tim Stories

Tim-Tim stories are based on the traditional stories that the slaves brought over from Africa. After a day working in the fields, they used to relax in the evenings by telling these stories. They are still told today but usually only in Creole and only in the rural areas. Many people in St Lucia are worried that story-telling is being replaced by television.

CALYPSOS

Calypsos are songs that tell a funny story about something that has recently happened. Calypso music is often played by steel bands to accompany limbo dancing. As part of the Carnival celebrations each year, there is a popular 'Calypso King' competition.

Earning a Living

People in St Lucia work in a wide range of different jobs. Some are teachers, lawyers, or police officers. Other people run shops, work in factories, fish or drive buses. But more people work in the banana and tourist industries than in any other type of job.

The Banana Industry

If you have ever eaten a banana it is very likely that it was grown in St Lucia. When the Europeans first came to the island, the most important crop was sugar cane. Slaves worked on the sugar plantations. But since the 1920s, bananas have become the main crop. Today, St Lucia has the largest banana crop in the Windward Islands. Nearly half of the money St Lucia makes from exports comes from bananas.

▼ Bananas are loaded on to the back of a truck at the Cul de Sac banana plantation.

CASE STUDY

Work on a Plantation

The people who work at the Cul de Sac Banana Plantation are always busy. Skilled cutters choose the best bananas to cut from the branches using razor-sharp machetes. The bananas are then washed. Once clean, they are packed up in boxes. Then they are taken to Castries port to be shipped.

▼ Some people in St Lucia have office jobs. This man works at the Ministry of Education.

▲ The bananas are washed carefully before they are packed into boxes.

The bananas are picked when they are green so that they can ripen on their long journey. They are packed in boxes on the plantation and transported to the harbour at Castries, where they are loaded on to the weekly banana boat. Ten days later, they are on supermarket shelves all over the world.

Working in Factories

Factories are also providing an increasing number of jobs in St Lucia. Several factories have been built around Vieux Fort. Most of these are owned by companies in other countries, but they do provide work for local people making clothes and toys. Foreign companies build factories in St Lucia because they can pay low wages here.

▲ These skilled sewing-machinists are working in an underwear factory in Castries.

◀ A fisherman mends his net. The fishing industry provides some jobs in St Lucia, but there are fewer fish than there used to be.

Working in Tourism

St Lucia is well known for its sandy beaches and agreeable climate, so it is no surprise that the island has become a popular place for holidaymakers to visit. The tourist industry provides a large number of jobs in St Lucia. Waiters, porters, and hotel and restaurant staff are all needed to keep the tourist industry booming. Tourism also creates work for local people who sell souvenirs to visitors.

But not everyone in St Lucia has a job. Many jobs are not regular and people have to do odd jobs here and there to make ends meet. Once a week, people queue for jobs loading the banana boat when it comes in.

▼ The loading of banana boats in Castries harbour provides casual work for some people.

Religion and Festivals

The French brought Roman Catholicism to St Lucia. Today, 90 per cent of St Lucians are Roman Catholics. Religion is very important here.

Christmas

One big celebration in St Lucia is Christmas. The religious side of Christmas is very important and people go to Midnight Mass. Each year, there is a large Carol Festival, at which choirs from all over the island come together to sing. St Lucians also celebrate Christmas with parties and special food, including Caribbean Christmas cake. This is made from fruit soaked in rum for several days, sometimes weeks. On Christmas Day, people go out to visit friends and family and exchange gifts. Although the weather is hot at Christmas time, people send each other cards with scenes showing snowy landscapes and decorate their homes with fir trees.

▼ **Leaving church after Sunday communion.**

Going to church is an ▶ **important part of every Sunday.**

Carnival

The highlight of the year in St Lucia is Carnival, which is usually held a few days before Lent. Children get very excited just before the Carnival and spend the weeks leading up to it making their costumes. Carnival is a mixture of European and African traditions. Everyone really gets into the spirit of Carnival, wearing brightly coloured costumes and dancing to the music. There are even contests with prizes for the best costumes.

St Lucia's National Day

St Lucy's Day, on 13 December, is St Lucia's national day. It was on this day that Christopher Columbus, an Italian explorer, was supposed to have arrived on the island. But most people now believe that Columbus never actually set foot on St Lucia.

FESTIVALS AND HOLIDAYS

1 January	New Year's Day
22 Feb	Independence Day
1 May	Labour Day
29 June	St Peter's Day (fishermen's festival)
7 August	Emancipation Day
13 December	St Lucy's Day

◀ **Ice cream is a real treat after church.**

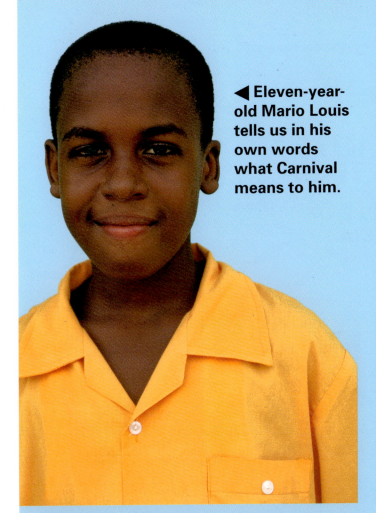

◀ **Eleven-year-old Mario Louis tells us in his own words what Carnival means to him.**

Carnival Time!

'Carnival takes place every year in St Lucia. It is always held just before Lent. Carnival is a lot of fun and everyone gets excited. Lots of different bands play music on big trucks, and people follow the trucks in beautiful costumes. Everyone jumps up (dances) and sings songs.

'Lots of people pay to join Carnival bands, so they can be part of the show. But some people just wait for the band to parade by and join in. There are three main towns in St Lucia where the Carnival is held – Castries, Vieux Fort and Soufrière. Some people jump up in the parade in Castries one day, in Vieux Fort the next, and in Soufrière on the last day. Then they go back to work when it's all over.'

▼ **Carnival is always very colourful in St Lucia.**

Topic Web
THE PEOPLE OF ST LUCIA

MUSIC
- Exploring rhythm
- Making sounds
- Percussion instruments

ART AND CRAFT
- Colours
- Textures of materials

R.E.
- Special days
- Carnival
- Christianity

HISTORY
- Researching slavery
- Migrations of people
- Researching colonialism
- Origins of carnival

GEOGRAPHY
- Tourism
- Types of weather and their advantages and disadvantages
- Types of food grown in different countries

DESIGN AND TECHNOLOGY
- Costume design
- Building materials

MATHS
- Currency
- Simple statistics

P.E./DANCE/ DRAMA
- Masquerade

SCIENCE
- Sound
- Nutritional value of food

ENGLISH
- Library skills
- Calypso

Extension Activities

R.E.
- Study how different people celebrate religious festivals.

GEOGRAPHY
- Look at the similarities and differences between St Lucia and your community.
- Draw a flow chart showing the journey of a banana, from the plantation to the supermarket.

DESIGN AND TECHNOLOGY
- Plan a school carnival.

ENGLISH
- Write a letter to a St Lucian penpal. Think about the things you would like them to know about your school day. What do you think might be different?
- Find out about Calypso and make up your own songs.

SCIENCE
- Cook a St Lucian meal.

P.E./DANCE/DRAMA
- Create your own Carnival dance.

MUSIC
- Make some simple Carnival instruments.

MATHS/INFORMATION TECHNOLOGY
- Using the exchange rate on page 5, work out the cost of a pint of milk, a small loaf of bread and a packet of tea in $ECs.
- Make graphs or pie charts from the statistics in the fact boxes.
- Produce some of these graphs or pie charts using computer software.

ART AND CRAFT
- Examine the colours and textures that can be used to create a Carnival costume.

Glossary

Breeze blocks Building bricks made from material left over from furnaces.

Carnival A fair just before Lent celebrated by Roman Catholics all over the world, usually with a procession.

Commonwealth A voluntary association of 53 countries, many of them former British colonies.

Co-operative A business that is owned and run jointly by its members, with all profits shared equally among them.

Galvanized iron Iron that has been coated with a layer of zinc to stop it rusting.

Lent A period 40 days before Easter in the Christian calendar.

Limbo dancing When a dancer bends backwards to pass under a pole. Sometimes the pole almost touches the ground.

Migrated Travelled from one place to another.

Plantations Large farms where one crop is grown and is usually exported.

Roman Catholicism The branch of the Christian Church headed by the Pope.

Slaves People who are the property of another person.

Suburbs Districts or communities on the outskirts of a town or city.

Veranda A roofed gallery or terrace around the front or side of a house.

Further Information

Non-fiction:

The Landscape of St Lucia by Alison Brownlie (Wayland, 1998)

Living in St Lucia Pupil's Book by Vincent Bunce and Wendy Morgan (Cambridge University Press, 1996). Also available to complement this title are a teacher's resource book, and a set of twelve A3 photocards.

Fiction:

My Grandpa and the Sea by Katherine Orr (Carolrhoda Books Inc., Minneapolis, 1990). Available from Worldaware.

Photopacks:

Focus on Castries, St Lucia by Vincent Bunce, James Foley, Wendy Morgan and Steve Scoble (Geographical Association/ Worldaware, 1997).

Go Bananas A photo-based activity pack focusing on the journey of a banana (Oxfam, 1990).

Audio-visual resources:

BBC Radio: Notes on Castries, St Lucia. Ten, 15-minute radio programmes.

Our Place: the Harveys – a 20-minute video produced by Worldaware.

Software:

Castries, St Lucia: a Contrasting Locality – a floppy-disk based software package (Worldaware, 1997).

Useful addresses:

For school links with St Lucia contact:
The Ministry of Education and Culture, (Primary), Castries, St Lucia, West Indies.

Oxfam, (Education), 274 Banbury Road, Oxford OX2 7DZ. Tel: 01865 311311.

The St Lucia Tourist Board, 421a Finchley Road, London NW3 6HJ. Tel: 0171 431 3675.

Worldaware, 31–35 Kirby Street, London EC1N 8TE. Tel: 0171 831 3844.

Index

Page numbers in **bold** refer to photographs.